The Reflections of My Labradoodle

A Coloring Book

DOGGY LANGUAGE

There's an entire language devoted to dogs; this language is known as Doggo Lingo. It's how your dog speaks and thinks. It's a fun, positive celebration of dogs.

Doggo	Doggos come in a variety of sizes ranked by the size of their bork (bark). They range from the tiny yapper to a diminutive pupper, an average-sized doggo, and the biggest woofers and boofers.
Longboi	A long-bodied dog such as a greyhound.
Floofer/Fluffer	A very fluffy dog such as a Samoyed or Pomeranian.
Thicc boi	A chubby dog – more to love.
Smol boi	A little yapper.
Woofer	A big dog.
Loaf	A dog, slightly overweight, which resembles a loaf of bread.
Pupper	A puppy.
Heckin' bamboozled	Sometimes you bamboozle the dog, sometimes the dog bamboozles you. Heck.
Do me a frighten	When a doggo is worried, scared or confused, potentially in the presence of borks or woofers.
Doin' me a	Having an action performed on oneself.
Bamboozle	A deceiving trick.
Awoo!	Howling.
Hooman	A human being.

DOGGY LANGUAGE

Heck, h*ck	The curse work in doggo lingo
Blep/Blop	When your pupper is tired and his tongue hangs out just a little bit.
Mlem	Doing a lick. Not to be confused with a gentle blop.
Bork	Barking his little head off. All doggers can bork.
Boof	Not quite a bork, not quite a sneeze; it's the small huffy sound of a dog who's getting ready to bork..
Maximum borkdrive	This is otherwise known as the zoomies, when your doggo is going so fast they're just a blur.
Chimken	Chicken.
Fren/frend	Friend
Henlo	Hello
Snoot	The nose always knows, and the snoot was made for booping.
Boop!	Touching your pet on the nose. Frequently accompanied by saying 'boop!'
Good Boi	There are no bad boys.

Me and the hooman and the new fren went for a walk. And we saw other woofers and I jumped into a mud puddle. Awoo!

About My Dog

Dog's Name:

Date of Birth:

Breed:

Colour:

Gender:

Adoption Date:

Weight:

Breeder:

Microchip No:

Registration No:

Rabies:

Neutered/Speyed:

If you're lucky...

A Labradoodle will come into your life,

...steal your heart and change everything!

BrightView
ACTIVITY BOOKS
COPYRIGHT © 2020

Some say a dog's life is easy...no worries, no taxes. I say, walk a mile in my shoes. That reminds me, I took your shoe.

SORRY, HOOMAN!

Photo

WE ARE AT THE PARK BUT THE HOOMAN SAYS IT'S TIME TO LEAVE

THIS DOESN'T MAKE SENSE BECAUSE THEY CAN'T CATCH ME

AWOO!

My dog does this amazing thing where he just exists and makes my whole life better because of it

Hello frens.
Today has been a great day to think about my accomplishments.
Here they are.

ZOOMIES OF THE SPEEDY VARIETY
MAXIMUM SNOOZLES
CHASING BRUCE THE SQUIRREL
BORKED AWAY ALL EVILDOERS
ATE A WORM
SPAT OUT THE WORM
SNUGGLED WITH MY STUFFED FREN, LEROY, ON THE HOOMAN'S BED.

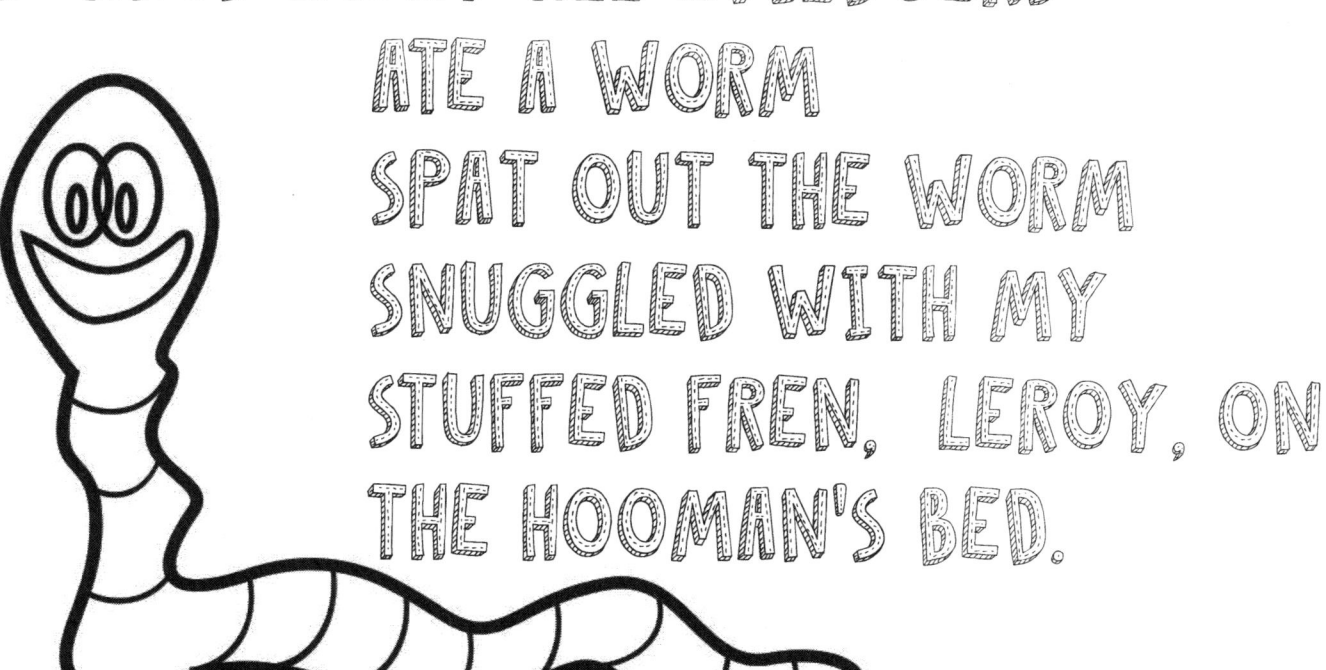

Dogs are like potato chips.
It's hard to have just one

The hooman yawned while having lunch, and in a split second, my floofer fren, Timbo, from next door stole a French fry. I AM WILDLY IMPRESSED!

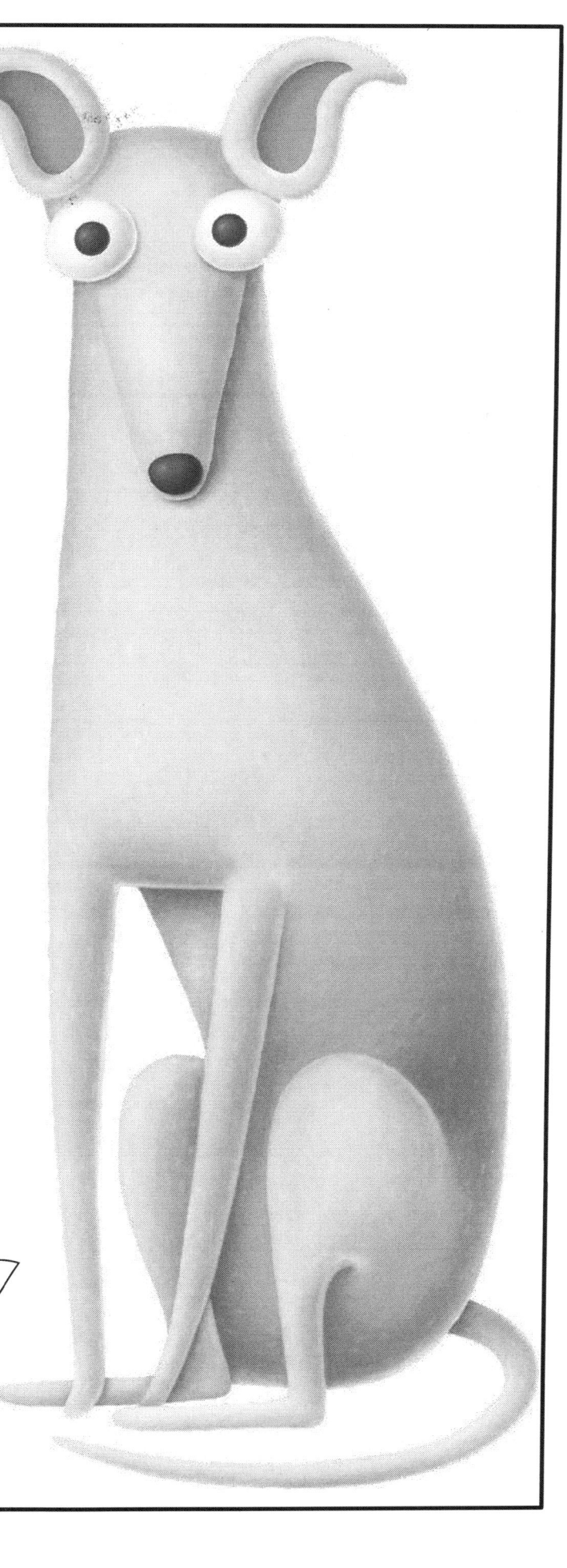

Dogs are God's way of apologizing for your relatives

MY EAR FLAP IS INSIDE OUT AND MY HOOMAN IS NOT HOME TO FIX IT

I HAVE GRRBORKED! ALERT LEVEL RED

Noise has woken me. Possible causes...
...world ending
...no other possibilities
...definite catastrophe
...wake the hooman!

NOW!

Photo

MY STUFFED FREN, LEROY, IS A VERY GOOD LISTENER. I TOLD HIM ABOUT MY IDEA FOR A DOG COAT WITH BIG POCKETS FOR CHIMKIN AND PEANUT BUTTER.

HE SAID THAT WAS HECKIN' BRILLIANT!

Dogs are the role model for being alive

JUST GIVE ME A LONG HALLWAY OF SHINY WOOD WITH SOME CHIMKIN AT THE END

AND I'LL SHOW YOU SOME IMPRESSIVE SKATING

A dog does not think much about what he is doing.
He just does what feels right

THE SMOL HOOMAN NEIGHBOR CAME OVER AFTER SCHOOL TO GET ME TO EAT THEIR HOMEWORK

HAPPY TO OBLIGE

BUT I'LL NEED PERSUADING

I LOVE CHEESE BY THE WAY

Dogs have personality.
Personality goes a long way

The mailman left a box
at the front door
It smells like peanut butter

I'm trying my best
to remain calm,
but I think it's for me

GRR! AWOOOOO... BOOF!

IN HAPPINESS

A new week is upon us....
Or so the hooman tells me.
Hooman time constructs do me a bamboozle. I prefer to break it down into snoozes, non snoozes and........

MAXIMUM BORKDRIVE

Photo

THE HOOMAN AND THE HOOMAN'S FREN HAVE GOT ALL DRESSED UP AND THEY'RE GOING OUT. I DON'T SEEM TO BE INVITED. THE GOOD NEWS IS, I JUMPED ON THEM BOTH, SO THEY HAVE PIECES OF ME TAGGING ALONG. AWOO!

I call my dog Egypt because he leaves a pyramid in each room

We have new neighbors & they have a new pupper

I AM SO EXCITED!!

I shall take my stuffed fren, Leroy to make frens

MY TAILS A WAGGIN'

Dogs do speak but only to those who listen

MY SQUEAKER TOY, PAULINE THE PINK PIG, IS STUCK UNDER THE FRIDGE.

I AM HECKIN BAMBOOZLED ON HOW TO RESCUE IT

My little dog — a heartbeat at my feet

I HAVE JUST COMPLETED MY MY SECURITY LAP AROUND THE HOUSE

ALERT LEVEL IS GREEN

READY FOR SNOOZLES IN MY HOOMAN'S BED

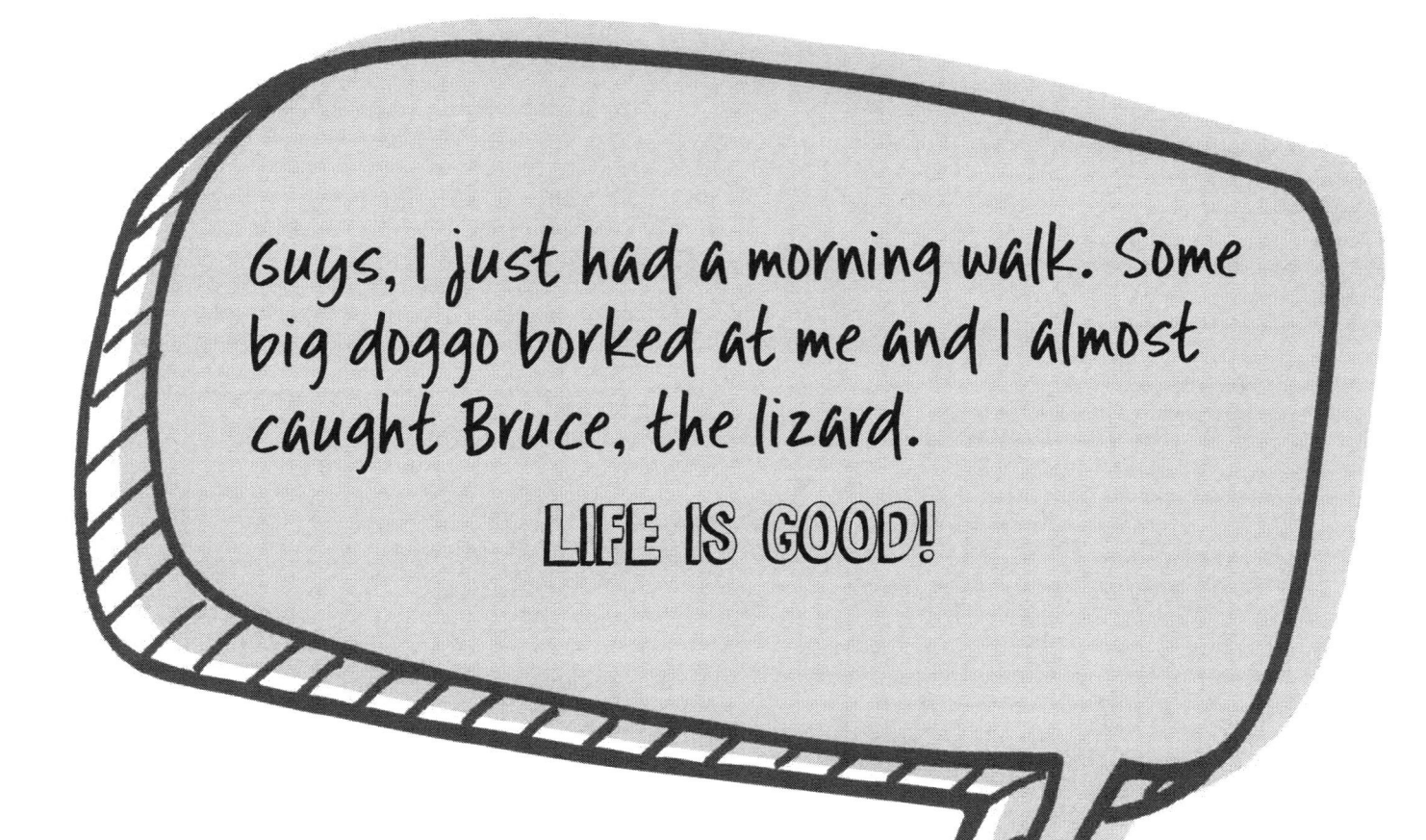

Guys, I just had a morning walk. Some big doggo borked at me and I almost caught Bruce, the lizard.

LIFE IS GOOD!

Photo

THAT PESKY CAT FROM NEXT DOOR SNUCK UP ON ME WHEN I WAS HAVING A SNOOZLE ON THE COUCH.

DID ME A HECK OF A FRIGHTEN!

GRR

I'LL BE READY NEXT TIME

Handle every situation like a dog.
If you can't eat it or play with it,
just pee on it

MANY HAVE TOLD ME WHAT A GOOD BOI I AM

AND LET'S SAY THEY ARE ABSOLUTELY RIGHT

I'D LIKE SOME CHEESE HOOMAN

No matter how many years we get with our dogs, it's never long enough

The night snoozle is here again. I have gathered my stuffed frens, Leroy & Alistair and they are safe in the hooman's bed.

THEY ARE AFRAID OF THE DARK

Some days you're the dog;
some days, you're the hydrant

Just finished the afternoon snoozle, and my schedule is wide open until dinner time when I will perform the

SPEEDY ZOOMIES!

I have been programming my hooman. Every time they give me food, I bork. Eventually, every time I bork, they will give me food.

I WANT CHEESE!

photo

I PRETENDED THAT I NEEDED TO GO THE BATHROOM

BUT I ONLY WANTED TO FEEL THE WIND ON MY NOGGIN

Every dog has his day, unless he loses his tail, then he has a weak-end

I HAVE TWO SPEEDS FOR WALKING

FASTER THAN YOU & COMPLETELY IMMOBILE (DRAGGING SPEED)

OF COURSE SOME PEANUT BUTTER OR A GOOD STICK COULD CHANGE THAT!

Every snack you make, every meal you bake.
Every bite you take, I'll be watching you

I GOT THE MAJORITY OF MY WORK DONE...
BETWEEN THE MORNING AND AFTERNOON SNOOZLES

But my hooman is cooking chimkin and I just know there will be some for me.

I wiggled a little bit....
just reminding her that
I am a good boi guard dog

My dog winks at me sometimes...
And I always wink back just in case
it's some kind of code

I am several hours into my shift guarding Pauline my squeaker pig

While I was there the fridge made some new crunch water

SOOTHED MY HECKIN' BROW

Bruce, the lizard, is staring at me through the screen door. "Bring it on, young fella."

DOIN' ME A FRIGHTEN!

Photo

I HAVE COMPLETED THE MORNING SECURITY LAP AROUND THE HOUSE

ALERT LEVEL GREEN

I AWAIT YOUR HUGS & CUDDLES

I LOVE CUPCAKES !

I wonder if other dogs think poodles are members of a weird religious cult

I JUST SAW SOME DOGGOS ON THE TV. I BORKED, GRBORKED AND BOOFED TO SHOW MY SUPPORT!

The great pleasure of a dog is that you may make a fool of yourself with him...

THE HOOMAN HAS JUST COME HOME...

HE'S BEEN GONE FOR WEEKS!!!!!!!!!!!!!!!

In his absence, I have gathered all the shoes and redistributed them around the house.

IT'S MY DUTY!

Dogs are such agreeable friends.
They ask no questions,
they pass no criticisms

MY HOOMAN HAS BOUGHT A NEW SOFA AND I'M NOT ALLOWED TO SNOOZLE ON IT.

I HAVE NO IDEA WHY BUT THIS SHALL BE REMEDIED

I WILL SLOWLY CLIMB UP ONE PAW AT A TIME.

NO ONE WILL EVER NOTICE!

Hooman gave me an extra long hug and direct eye contact. These are heckin' signals. We're on the same page.

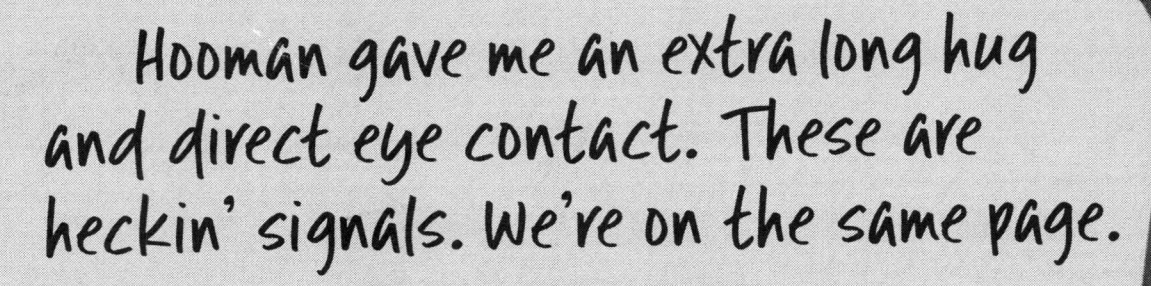

I FEEL CHIMKIN COMING!

Photo

BARK!!

A nice hooman came to the house to fix the spinny machine. It was doin' me a frighten.

To thank him, I stayed close to him the whole time

WOOF! GRR

My sunshine doesn't come from the skies.
It comes from the love that's in my dogs eyes

MY HOOMAN IS HOSTING A DINNER PARTY TONIGHT

AND it's MY joB to GReet all the Guests

CALMLY ... NO JUMPING!!!

THIS IS NOT POSSIBLE

I SHALL SEEK THE HELP OF MY STUFFED FREN, CHRISTMAS TURKEY

AWOO!!

There is no psychiatrist in the world like a puppy licking your face

SOMETHING HAS WOKEN ME UP
IT'S THAT PESKY CAT, BORIS

> I HAVE GATHERED MY STUFFED FREN, ALISTAIR THE CROCODILE AND PREPARED FOR EXTENDED SNOOZLES

A dog will always be happier to see you than any person ever will

I HEAR A DOGGO BORKING IN THE DISTANCE

It is my duty to respond so that all the other doggos know I heard the initial borking

IT'S JUST GOOD MANNERS!

!*WOOF*!

The hooman said we could go on a car ride tomorrow when he gets home. I'm so happy, I can't even snooze.

TAIL IS WAGGING SO FAST!

Photo

SOME CRUNCH WATER FELL OUT OF THE FREEZER I JUST HAD TO LICK IT

NOW MY THONGUE IST FROZEN

If our dog doesn't like you,
we probably won't either

I HAVE MISPLACED MY NEW FREN, CHRISTMAS TURKEY

ALERT LEVEL RED

NEVER MIND I WAS LYING ON HIM THE WHOLE TIME

ALERT LEVEL GREEN

Don't let the dogs out
no matter what they tell you

A Lot Happened On Our Morning Walk

> I found a perfectly good chimkin leg in the neighbor's trash, but the hooman wouldn't let me have it.

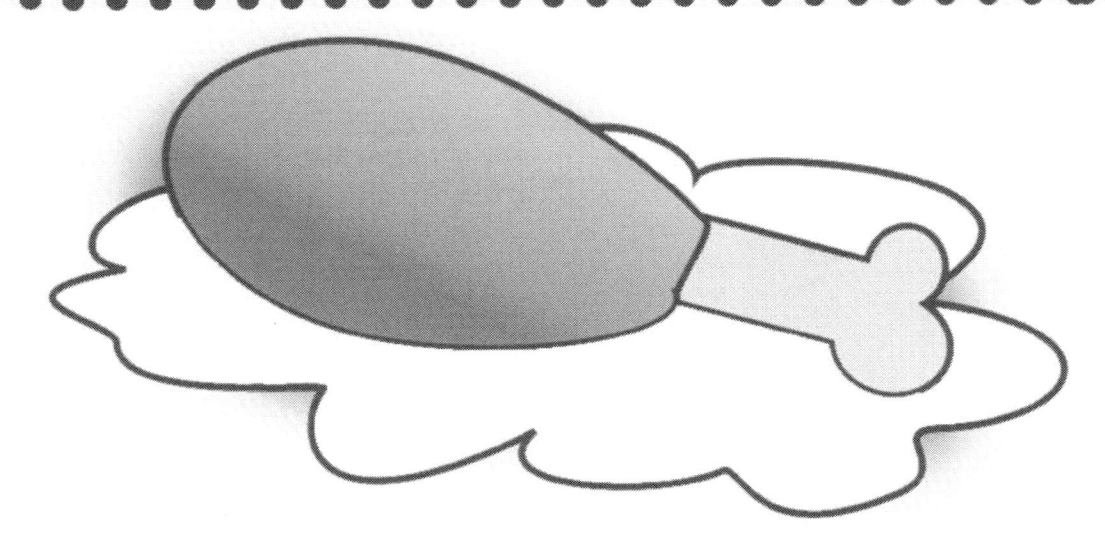

THERE WAS ALSO A VERY SCARY PLASTIC BAG

Dogs are better than humans because they know but do not tell

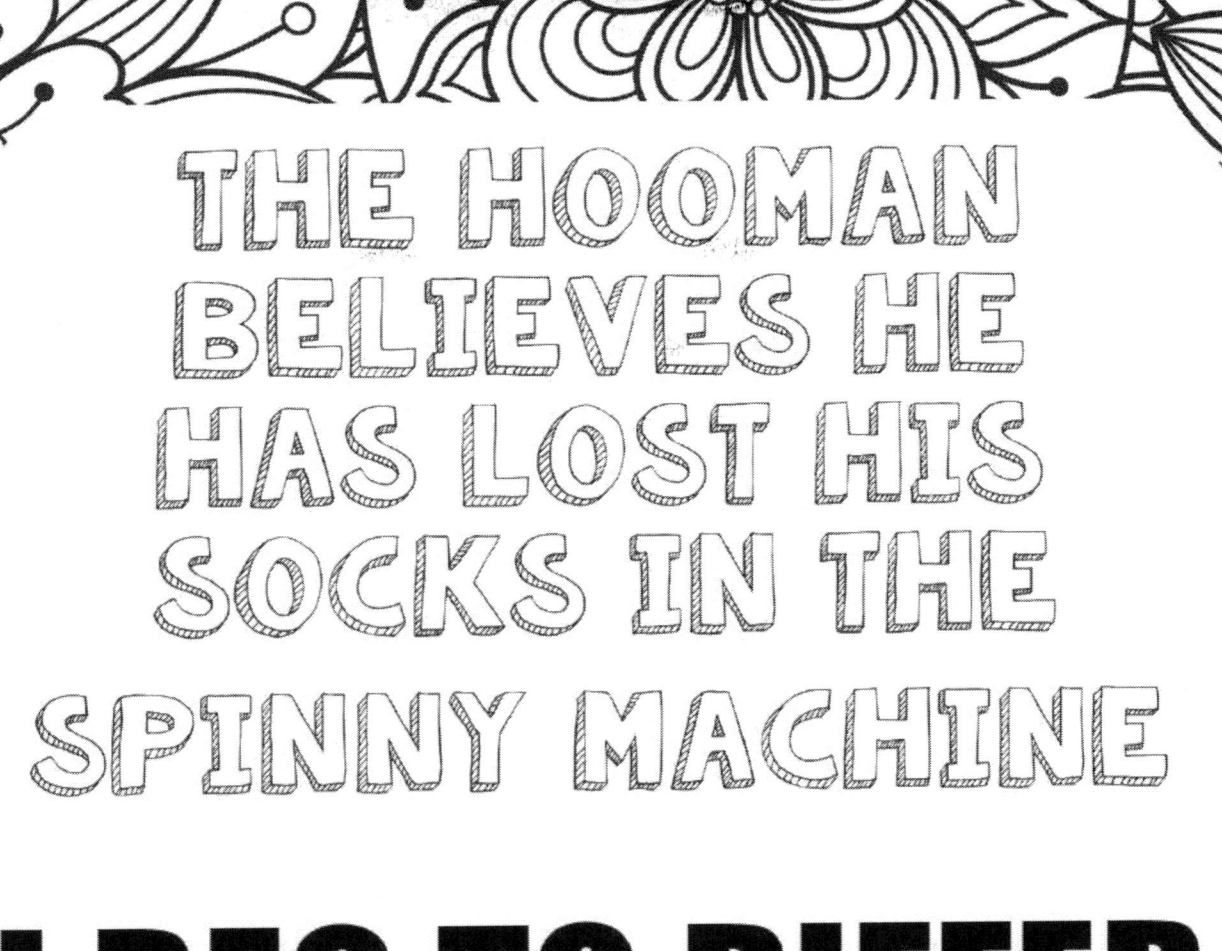

THE HOOMAN BELIEVES HE HAS LOST HIS SOCKS IN THE SPINNY MACHINE

I BEG TO DIFFER
I steal them way before that

Hardwood floors are not ideal for doin' the zoomies. No traction anywhere. This situation needs to be remedied, hooman.

EAR FLAPS STUCK IN THE COUCH.!

Photo

TODAY I STOLE A WHOLE SLAB OF CHEESE

It took several house loops before the hooman retrieved it

I really love the sound of my dog snoring

I ACCIDENTALLY STOLE THE TOILET PAPER AND DECORATED THE WHOLE HOUSE

MY HOOMAN WAS WELL PLEASED!

Scratch a dog and you'll find a permanent job

I JUST WOKE UP FROM MY AFTERNOON POWER SNOOZLE

WHICH IS AFTER THE MORNING SNOOZLE

AND BEFORE MY NIGHT TIME SNOOZLE

I CAN'T KEEP UP WITH MY DAY!

My dog is half pit-bull, half poodle.
Not much of a watchdog, but a vicious gossip

DURING MY NIGHT TIME SNOOZLE I DREAMED THAT I DUG UP A BOX IN THE GARDEN & IT WAS FILLED WITH CHEESE

TODAY, I WILL TEST THIS OUT!

My most fancy tricks...
Snoozing, sit (a classic), the fetch, trot/advanced walk, roll, zoom (speedy), begging for chimkin.

SORTED BY DIFFICULTY!

Photo

I DRANK ALL THE WATER FROM MY BOWL BUT JUST NOW, IT IS FULL AGAIN

IT'S DOIN ME A FRIGHTEN

Everybody should have a shelter dog.
It's good for the soul

IF YOU HEAR A SINGLE **BORK** AND THEN A **BOOF** IT'S ONLY ME TESTING THE SAFETY OF THE HOUSEHOLD

other doggos may respond & then we have a chorus!

If it wasn't for puppies, some people would never go for a walk

Today, I did a zoom so speedy my ear flaps flew back

MY FLOOFER FREN FROM NEXT DOOR WAS WELL-IMPRESSED!

If you're uncomfortable around my dog,
I'm happy to lock you in the other room
when you come over

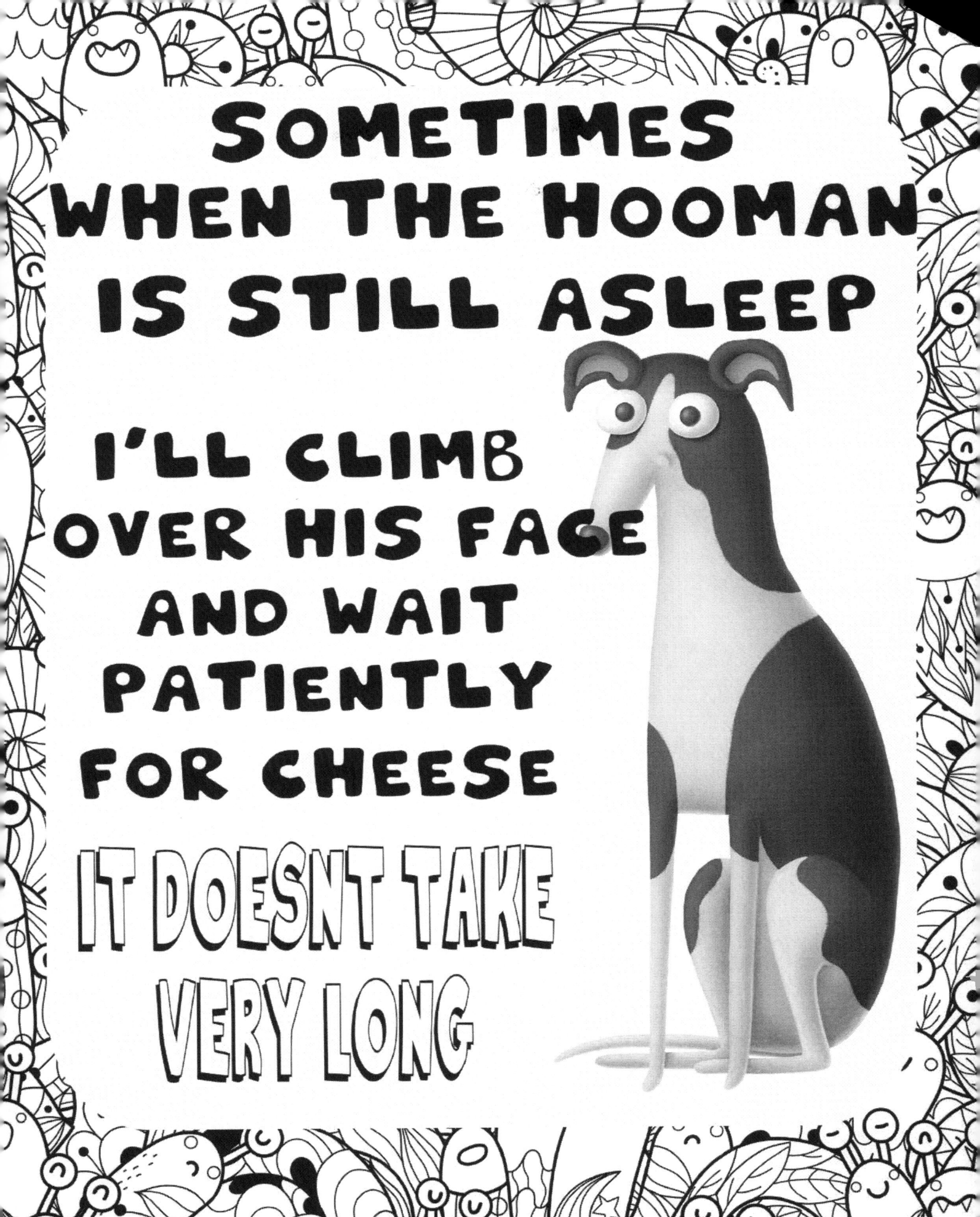

SOMETIMES WHEN THE HOOMAN IS STILL ASLEEP

I'LL CLIMB OVER HIS FACE AND WAIT PATIENTLY FOR CHEESE

IT DOESNT TAKE VERY LONG

Sometimes, I grrbork at the sky... in case anybody is listening.
You ever wake up in the middle of the night and think...why?

I NEED CHIMKIN!

Photo

I COLLECTED ALL OF MY BALLS & SHOWED MY NEW FREN, LEON HOW TO HOLD THEM ALL IN HIS MOUTH

He's only little — He could only do one

A dog has no use for fancy cars, big homes, or designer clothes. A stick will do just fine

SOMETIMES, MY HOOMAN WILL LIFT UP MY EAR FLAP AND SCRATCH MY NOGGIN

GYY

THIS IS COMPLETELY UNNECESSARY

When I needed a hand, I found your paw

Sometimes, I make a small **BOOF** to let my hooman know I need to go outside.

Then I just stand in the doorway & sniff the air

HECKIN BAMBOOZLED

Everyone thinks they have the best dog.
And none of them are wrong

MY THICKBOI
FREN THEODORE
FROM NEXT DOOR
STOLE THE SOCKS
I STOLE

HECKIN' RUDE

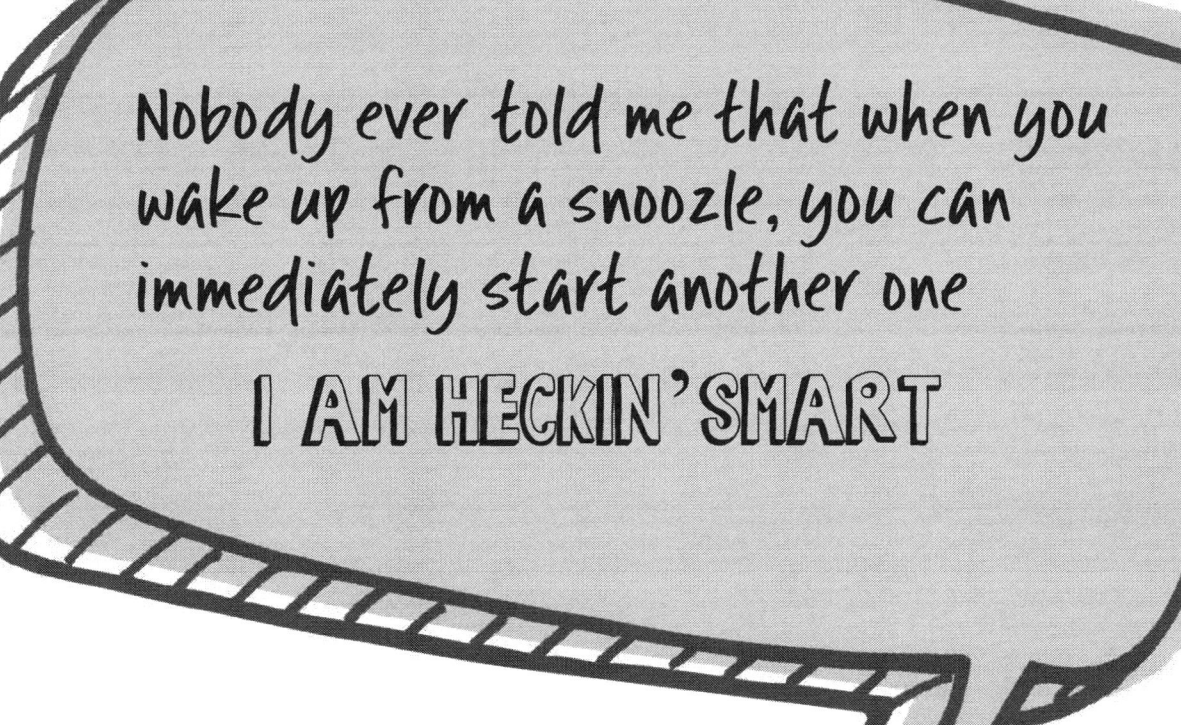

> Nobody ever told me that when you wake up from a snoozle, you can immediately start another one
>
> **I AM HECKIN' SMART**

Photo

THE HOOMAN HAS A NEW FREN OVER.

IF I AM IGNORED, I WILL NOTIFY THE FREN WITH A SERIES OF DISCRETE BORKS

> EITHER PAT MY NOGGIN OR GIVE ME PEANUT BUTTER

BORK BOOF GRR BORK

Dogs have a way of finding the people who need them, and filling an emptiness we didn't ever know we had

LET ME TELL YOU ABOUT MY BEST STUFFED FREN, JEREMY

HE'S MY BESTEST PAL

HE'S GOT A LONG SNOOT FLOPPY EAR FLAPS

HE AGREES WITH EVERYTHING I SAY

Whoever said that diamonds are a girl's best friend... Never owned a dog

MY TOP AGGRAVATIONS

BORIS, THE PESKY CAT

THE SPINNY MACHINE

LEASH TANGLES

CRUNCH WATER

INSIDE OUT EAR FLAPS

STICKS THAT BREAK

TAKE NOTE, HOOMAN

Some people don't understand
why my dog means so much to me.
That's ok. My dog does

SOMETHING HAS WOKEN ME FROM MY AFTERNOON SNOOZLE

AWOO!!!

CHIMKIN!!

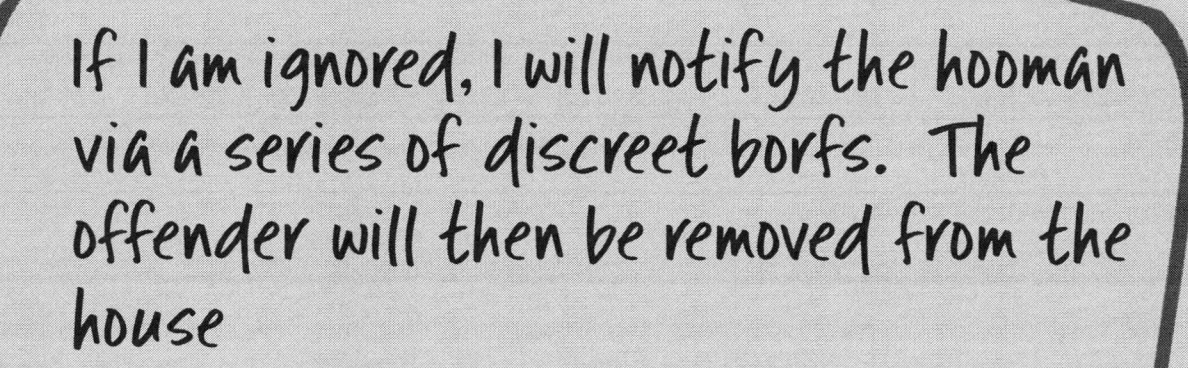

If I am ignored, I will notify the hooman via a series of discreet borfs. The offender will then be removed from the house

IMMEDIATELY!

Photo

DURING MY NIGHT SNOOZLE, I DREAMT ABOUT A PEANUT BUTTER LEASH

MY MORNING WALK IS GOING TO BE

AMAZING

Stop telling me he's just a dog.
My dog has more personality, integrity,
empathy and loyalty than most people I know.
He's family!

I HAVE NO PLANS TODAY
JUST SNOOZLES AND SNACKS

I CANCELLED MY PLANS WITH MY FLOOFER FREN, TIMBO ABOUT HOW TO DO

MAXIMUM ZOOMIES

ON HARD WOOD FLOORS

A dog will always be happier to see you than any person ever will

DID I EVER TELL YOU

I love you hooman

```
┌─────────────────────────────────┐
│                                 │
│                                 │
│                                 │
│             Photo               │
│                                 │
│                                 │
│                                 │
└─────────────────────────────────┘
```

Made in United States
Orlando, FL
03 November 2022